SUMMARY
MONEY MASTER THE GAME

Summary and Action Guide,

7 Simple Steps to Financial Freedom

By Jonathan Chase

TABLE OF CONTENTS

INTRODUCTION

I want to thank you and congratulate you for downloading this book.

This book contains proven steps and strategies on how to use Tony Robbins' concepts of money management to build your investment and savings portfolio.

If you want to retire from your average nine to five job, if you want to be able to enjoy life without the worry and anxiousness associated with living paycheck to paycheck and hand to mouth, Tony's proven strategies for saving and developing investments are instrumental achieving your financial goals.

This book summarizes Robbins' amazing 688-page book into segments of readable content.

- You don't have to read his whole book to gain the wisdom to obtain your Financial Freedom.

- Following the concepts outlined in this summary will enable you to effectively build your investment portfolio.

- Utilizing the information inside will change the way you think about saving and spending your money.

- Tony's inspirational message will help you understand not to work for money but let your money work for you.

Thanks again for downloading this book, I hope you enjoy it!

STEP 1: SHIFT FROM CONSUMER TO OWNER

Tony Robbins' best-selling book says that **step one to true financial freedom is making the shift from consumer to owner by becoming an investor.** Too many people have the notion that speaking of money is shameful and secretive. Tony breaks through these barriers as he believes we don't receive the education about money, because of the taboo factors, that is needed to control it properly. This lack of education is hurting people and depleting their progress towards the goal of financial freedom. Instead of taking the initiative and making our money work for us, we work for our money.

We will never gain true financial freedom by working for "the man" and counting on "the man" to fill our wallets and our retirement funds. If you have a good company pension, hang on to this employer. It is increasingly rare to receive a pension from a corporation, even though many employers offer and contribute to their 401(k) retirement account, employees must also fund the maximum allowable deduction from their salary.

Counting on your employer to provide a pension is just the very beginning of proper investment strategies to ensure your comfortable retirement. Just like social security is not going to give you enough assets to have a comfortable retirement income, neither is your corporate pension. Even your social security checks, your corporate pension, and your 401(k) will likely not provide the cash flow to anticipate your needs at retirement age.

Things change when you retire. The large house that was great for a growing family is now an energy eater with high utility bills and prolonged maintenance costs. The individual that had wonderful health through his sixties may have a heart attack or stroke in his seventies, meaning that health care costs just skyrocketed and take a much bigger slice of the monthly income. A lot of the newer drugs that are needed to care for complicated medical problems are not available through insurance plans. These drugs can be upwards of $500 for a monthly dose, eating deeply into the monthly budget. Car insurance rates double after the age of 70. Vehicle licenses must be renewed in person, and the person must pass the vision and hearing tests. If the tests are failed, one might have to purchase hearing aids and glasses, neither of which are likely not covered by most insurance policies or Medicare. These are high ticket items that may cost in the thousands of dollars to the consumer.

One of the biggest lies that rob people of the ability to control their money is propagated by Hollywood. Hollywood promotes living well as the end result of exceptional earnings. People buy into the Hollywood hype that having money means spending money conspicuously in order to prove they are a success in the world. Hollywood has a lot of "big hat, no cattle" people that are living paycheck to paycheck, and hand to mouth, but have misplaced priorities on how to work their money to increase their net worth.

These people see money as a way to show their worth, but the bottom line is they have a negative net worth. They are upside down on their mortgage, have no lasting assets, and live a lucrative lifestyle as long as the big paychecks are rolling into the coffers. When the paychecks stop rolling, the Hollywood spender is bankrupt, because they have no investment plan, no savings, and even possibly a leased house and vehicle, all to be returned to the creditors.

Tony insists that to handle money properly, gaining the right perspective about money is imperative. The correct attitude towards money is to master the money game by investing in yourself instead of expensive toys and high end vehicles or homes. Although these toys and luxurious wrappings will bring temporary happiness, and maybe even joy for the right person, these emotions are fleeting. The happiness will disappear when the newness of the purchase wears off. There will be no happiness if the house is foreclosed or the vehicle repossessed because of mismanagement of funds. This temporary boost of the happiness factor will not result in a permanent satisfaction, or financial stability, or control of the impulse spending.

Money mastery, according to Tony Robbins, takes a shift in attitude and a commitment to learning skills that are difficult to comprehend and take effort to understand and utilize. To thoroughly comprehend the value of money you must master these three fundamental concepts:

1. You must have a cognitive understanding of money

    a. Knowing information about money is not the same as utilizing good financial concepts in your goals for your life. A cognitive understanding requires using the knowledge internally instead of reading and filing the information to use in the future "someday." Having a cognitive understanding of money requires using the information on a daily basis of how to budget money, how to save money, and how to invest money for profitable returns and economic assurance.

    You must have an emotional understanding that money doesn't buy happiness, joy or stability. Fulfilling emotional desires by purchasing a houseful of things will not sustain happiness. Using money as a status symbol is indicative of immaturity in financial decisions and is detrimental to your personal and portfolio growth.

    b. In the emotional understanding stage of money management, you will have realized that you are conscious and capable of utilizing what you have learned. You will no longer have the desire for more, newer, or better but will understand that long term goals are more desirable than short term fixes to your emotional health. Emotional understanding of finances allows you to grow beyond the toddler expectation of "I want it, and I want it now!" Emotionally mature persons realize that long term gains are the wiser course of action and do not spend every dime they receive for temporary pleasures or items.

2. Total money mastery also requires the third understanding, physical mastery of money.

    a. The physical mastery concept is completed when repetition occurs. This means you have followed the concepts so thoroughly and often enough that it is no longer a conscious effort to save and invest, but instead a physical response to receiving money. In the physical mastery stage, money will no longer be "windfall" so therefore free from spending rules, instead "windfall" money is immediately deposited into savings as an automatic response. No shoe shopping, no electronic gadget shopping, no upgrading of the lifestyle, just an automatic response to increase the savings and investments accounts.

Saving and investing money are two sides of a coin. We need both sides of the coin to make the equation work. Just saving money isn't enough because it isn't making the money work for you. If you work hard all your life and just save the money in your mattress, in your crawl space, in the attic, or in a certificate of deposit at the local bank, your money will never work for you and create the financial freedom that you desire. Instead, invest your money in a portfolio of stocks, bonds, funds, annuities, property, gold and commodities.

1. Make a budget to see how much can be saved as savings can protect the family from catastrophe, bankruptcy, foreclosure, and depending on a government bailout. Savings is the key to financial security. The key to financial freedom is ensuring your money savings works for you.

    a. Figure your net worth today. Use this free net *worth calculator* (http://www.bankrate.com/calculators/smart-spending/personal-net-worth-calculator.aspx) to determine your exact financial standing. Robbins suggests comparing your net worth to others in your age and financial status category. *USA Today* has a handy tool for this configuration (http://www.usatoday.com/story/money/personalfinance/2015/01/31/motley-fool-net-worth-age/22415229). This comparison will help you see if you are on the upside and using money management concepts well, or on the downside, and spend too much of your income on frivolities. When it comes to money management, the best thing you can do is to be honest with yourself. You have too much to lose to not look at the charts and figures.

2. Cut back on everything to save money. This is your time of wealth accumulation. Use <u>Mint.com</u> as a good tool to track money so that you are aware where every penny goes. Mint is a free money tracking online software that links your checking account to bill paying, has visual charts and graphs to help you manage your money, and gives updates of your credit score. These are all helpful products under one umbrella website that is of no cost to you. With Mint, you will see exactly where your money is spent, how often you have late payments, what fees you are paying to your bank, how well you are managing your vehicle loans, and if a lower rate for your car insurance is available.

   a. Often people see the leftover from their budget as disposable income. This is counterproductive to realizing your financial goals of Financial Independence. To be serious retiring early and avoid being a slave to the nine to five grindstone, you need to realize you have no disposable income, only savings and investment opportunities.

3. Trim and trash every piece of fat from your spending to save as much as you possibly can. If you are not using internet for your primary business income, don't pay for it in an expensive bundled package from a cable company. Cable is not a necessary expense even in towns without television stations if you have an internet connection. Just about every network television show is available through internet access. To proj-

ect it to your television screen instead of a computer screen buy a Google Chromecast doggle, an Amazon tv doggle, or a Roku. All of these add ons to your television allow projection from the computer or phone to the television. They also provide Netflix, a subscription service that offers full seasons of television viewing and current movies for approximately $10 a month.

a. Carefully evaluate and assess every wasteful spending habit you have erroneously created in your budget. Consider if you are willing to give up new fashionable clothing in exchange for classic pieces that can be worn year to year. Take the clothing budget figure that wasn't spent to the investment account.

b. Is your gym membership really necessary? Are you using it five times a week? If you are not, you are wasting money. Analyze what you like about the gym and see if you can duplicate it at home. If you like a particular piece of equipment, purchase it for your home and use it there. Believe it or not, purchasing your own equipment will usually pay for itself within a year while saving on membership fees. Conversely, if your gym membership is a company perk, paid for by your insurance, or a free gift, use it more often. You need to take care of your physical health as much as your monetary health.

c. Look at eating out as a poor spending habit and change it to a once a month occasion. If you don't have time to cook, invest in a crock-pot and plan the evening meal before you leave for work in the morning.

   i. Drink protein shakes for at least one meal a day. They are fast, inexpensive, and help maintain your proper nutritional needs while giving you an easy meal preparation. Take the difference in what you spent last month in dining out and put it in the savings account.

ii. Develop a once a month meal plan or cooking plan. Team up with a friend to spend the day making freezer meals. Find ways to decrease your grocery budget while increasing your nutritional content. A family that dines together has been proven to weather calamities and crises much better than one who does not.

d. Closely analyze your food budget. The average family of four spends $700 a month on food and household products. How much of this spending could be reduced by coupon shopping? Coupons can be purchased online in bulk by researching coupon clipping services. These savings can be transferred to the savings and investments accounts.

i. Look to see if Costco, Sam's Club, and Amazon have programs that reduce your basic grocery costs and offer free delivery. Every time you can eliminate a trip to the store you have reduced your spending.

e. Cut lawn maintenance by planting slow growing grass or even a rock garden landscape. Paying someone for lawn maintenance is costly and could be earning you dividends and interest in an investment account.

i. Conversely, eliminate the maintenance or lawn service by doing the work yourself with a push mower, increasing your exercise while decreasing your budgetary costs. Place the money in savings.

f. Do you spend money weekly at the nail salon or beauty/barber shop? Can this be stretched to two weeks, or even not at all? This is another potential money sucker from your dedicated savings and investment portfolio. If you cut the manicures to once every two weeks, and a hair trim to once a month, a significant amount can go into the savings portfolio.

    i.   What are your other hidden weekly expenses? Do you drive through Starbucks or McDonalds each morning for breakfast coffee and a muffin? Buying a package of muffins and freezing them and brewing Starbucks coffee at home will cut that $8 a day habit to about $2. This leaves $6 a day to add to savings.

4.   Start as small as you have to, even at zero, but begin your investment account today with the minimum deposit, if necessary. Robbins suggests using *betterment.com* to begin investing because they have absolutely no minimum balance and they have low user fees. Putting off saving until you have "enough" to save will mean you will never reach your financial goals. Many successful savers will tell you that if you wait until you have the money to save, you will never have the money. Pay yourself first no matter what, and pay yourself consistently. The purpose of putting $5 a week in savings is to develop the habit. It takes 21 repetitive motions to develop an ingrained habit. Start your good habit of saving today, no matter how small the amount.

5.   Use and abuse the miracle of compound interest. Robbins relates the story of twin brothers that applied very different savings strategies in their life. William opened an investment account at age 20 and saved $4,000 annually for twenty years. James didn't start saving until he was 40, but also saved $4,000 annually, and contributed for twenty-five years. William, the early investor, saved $80,000 and received 10% annually in compound interest. James, the later investor, saved $100,000, and also received 10% in compound interest.

The end result was William had almost $2.5 million in his account, and James had only $400,000. The compound interest was the difference. The earlier you save the better your results will be, regardless of the amount that is contributed weekly, because of the effect of compound interest. More often contributions of smaller amounts are more important than big contributions just once a year. The addition of compound interest means the little deposits are accruing interest daily, while the large sum of money only accrues interest for a few days.

6. Eliminate all debt by using the snowball effect. The snowball effect involves listing every single debt you owe in order of descending balances. Don't make big payments on all of your balances. Consider instead making the minimum payments. Now you can use the extra cash left over to pay off one credit card or debt at a time. Start with the smallest balance, and pay it off immediately. Take the payment money you would have spent on this balance and apply it to the next balance on the list. Do this until you owe nothing, except for your home and primary residence. This will create a snowball effect for your debt, as you will be applying larger payments to each remaining balance owed at the top of the list.

   a. Evaluate whether your home loan and interest is working for you or against you. Is the deduction for interest keeping your tax deductions at the optimum level? If it is not, eliminate this interest, as it is money flowing out of your wallet. Pay off the mortgage and save the payment every month to the investment account.

7. Do not stop saving money even when times are hard. The consistent savings are your ticket to financial freedom. Don't cash in your ticket because you are struggling. Find a way to continue to save, even if you have to sell a beloved collection or special art piece. Even sell a family jewel or keepsake to save. Believe in yourself enough to consistently and repetitively invest in your future.

   a. Reduce your stuff in your home. Do you really need 108 place settings of china and silverware? Sell the surplus on eBay or Craigslist and add to your investment account.

b. How many televisions do you need? Shoes? Suits? Bedrooms? All of the maintenance of these items reduce your ability to save.

c. Look at the size of your home. Are you purchasing too much square footage? If you are a couple with no children, why do you need more than two bedrooms and two baths? Look at smaller homes with your desired features and consider trading down. A smaller home will use less utilities and take less furnishings. You can sell the excess furnishings and accessories for an addition to your savings account.

d. What about your hobbies? Do you have excess fabric, wood, tools, or cars? All of these assets can be liquidated to bolster your savings and investments account.

e. Make your savings and investments accounts more important than anything else that is your focus of your attention. This is the priority now for you and your family.

8. Tony suggests downloading his free app to make a plan to meet your financial goals. Get the Master the Game app here (https://financeapp.moneymasterthegame.com). This application gives you information on how to save, what to save, and the optimum tools to save money. This is a step-by-step guide to financial planning that is easy to use and to the point.

a. Are you on-track for your spending percentages? A family should be spending the following numbers on their monthly expenses:

i. Housing. 30% includes mortgage, insurance and taxes

ii. Food. 20% food and household needs

   iii.   Clothing. 10% clothing for all parties including diapers

   iv.   Transportation. 12% car, fees, tolls, maintenance, ins and fuel.

   v.   Medical. 12% co-pays, ins, and prescription costs.

   vi.   Savings. 10% never skimp here!

   vii.   Entertainment. 4% includes cable, internet, and going out.

   viii.   Just in case. 2% emergency on the spot money.

9. Consulting the save-more calculator (http://www.nytimes. com/interactive/2010/03/24/your-money/one-pct-more-calculator.html) will demonstrate the difference in your savings and investment balances by stepping up the game. When you see the money on an activity chart, you will realize where the extra purchases are located in your spending habits. This save-more calculator will challenge you to cut your spending to the bare bones. It will also give you a specific number from its calculations that you are capable of saving each month through careful monitoring of your money and spending habits. This amount will be a shock because this calculator doesn't care that you like Prada purses and can't resist their new line. Remember, when you buy a product you are lining their pockets with the money that could be yours.

Tony Robbins reiterates that our emotional investment in money is really a subconscious attempt to satisfy one of these basic needs:

- Our need for certainty, comfort and stability in our lives. We use money to buy a big house or a fancy car with all the bells and whistles, an outward symbol of comfort and stability. Internally this is only a temporary fix that drains our wallet and potential asset portfolio. Outwardly it looks good to the neighbors because they don't know that we've sacrificed our future returns to look good and have a wealthy appearance.

- ○ Stability is such a basic need that we will do anything to secure our comfort, even rob our future. Many people spend more than they can afford on a big house that also has high maintenance costs, just so they can look affluent to their peers.

- ○ A lot of spending is for things we don't want, to impress people we don't like, so that we can work forever to pay the debt we've incurred to give the impression of affluence or wealth. Break the cycle of spending to look good, instead look good because you don't spend, you save and invest in your own future.

- Our need for variety and uncertainty, or surprises in our lives. We use money to pump our adrenaline and alleviate our boredom with expensive impulse purchases. Later we are left with broken toys and an empty bank account.

- ○ Saving money can be a mundane experience if you allow it to become a chore in your mind. Change your attitude to the game mentality, where you want to beat the game of conspicuous consumption. Allow yourself to live comfortably. Be grateful for what you have. If you want to purchase an item, write yourself a letter as to why you want this purchase. Date the letter to yourself and give three reasons you believe this justifies robbing your future to reduce savings accumulation for this item. Put the letter away for 30 days. Take the letter back out and read it one month later to see if the reasons are still valid. If they are, give yourself permission to buy. If they are not, scrap the desire and the item from your wish list. You have now learned how to avoid impulse buys that wreck your budget.

- ○ Do you alleviate boredom by attending the movies each week? Going to the movies for a family of four is at least $50. Cut this to once a month, subscribe to Netflix at $10 a month, buy a popcorn popper, butter and popcorn, and you have saved $100 to put in the savings account. Make homemade pizza on movie night and save $25 more. Now you have $125 to save. Think creatively for ways to keep the enjoyment but lessen the expense of your family entertainments.

- ○ Go to zoos or museums on the free or reduced price days. They will be more crowded but just as enjoyable for your family. If your family adores looking at the cute monkeys at the zoo, purchase a family membership. This will give you access to your local zoo, and will give you admission to hundreds of zoos within the United States. Instead of taking your family on a resort vacation, take them on a zoo vacation when you travel. The cost will be considerably less but the satisfaction will be the same.

- Our need for significance by way of awards, education, and the need to be needed. We use money to gain advanced degrees that may not be useful in our chosen field of earnings. We use money to achieve awards in our chosen field by buying votes or updated equipment with bells and whistles that are not necessary. We use money to help pay bills for our entourage of followers, so we will be needed. All of these aforementioned money pits are to answer our emotional need to be "special."

  - ○ Pick a less expensive way to be special. Adopt a child with an orphanage by contributing $30 a month towards her school and healthcare expenses. Write her a letter every week. Send her a package once a month. This type of adoption has long term effects on her life and yours, because it creates a real relationship instead of an artificial adrenaline rush.

- Find places you can contribute in your local community. Your local animal shelter always has needs that a donor can fulfill, such as pet food, vet bills, caring for the animals by being a foster parent, or donating your time to cleaning cages and walking dogs or petting cats. These are much less expensive endeavors that create lasting relationships, networks, and friendships.

- Our need for love and connection. Some people buy this need by having a large group of followers. We all need connections. It is nice to say we wish we could live on a deserted island but not many people purchase deserted islands because of the need of love and connection. Sometimes we buy connections by lending people money, subconsciously realizing they will continue in our lives because we are supplying their needs.

  - Supply a real need instead by contributing to microbusinesses in India. One donation of a $125 sewing machine can change the future for a family of four that is headed by a widow or single mother.

  - Heifer Project International accepts donations of a family of rabbits or a goat to supply nutritional needs to poor citizens of underdeveloped countries. These are life changing contributions that give a protein source and a product to sell, giving the family a boost in physical, emotional, and mental health.

- Our need for growth. If you're not growing, you're dying. We always need to be growing, learning, and achieving new things. A dormant person is a depressed person on the road to decay and death.

  - Pick a new subject and dive into the free resources offered by the internet and your local library. Become an expert on the subject and write an eBook. Sell this eBook and use the profits for investing and savings.

- Our need for contribution, or giving back. One of the most essential elements of happiness is having an attitude of gratitude. We all need to realize that we are rich in blessings, and must give back to the world as a way of expressing our gratitude for our richness.

  o Look closely in the mirror at your reflection.

  o What are you doing to give back to the world around you? Change your lifestyle from taker to giver.

  o Are you giving locally? Do you have a local charity that knows you by name? This can be a church, a civic organization, or a humanitarian need. Volunteer and support it so well that the other participants know your name and how to contact you.

  o Are you giving nationally? Is there a national organization that you are supporting through your presence, your service, or your giving? Research and see what you can do. Everybody needs help sometime and why not grow yourself by contributing by helping those in need.

  o Are you giving internationally? Is your world limited by the 3 square miles around your place of residence? Expand your presence in the world by giving internationally to an organization of your choosing.

  o What is your personal contribution to make the world a better place for the next generation? Examine your priorities and determine where you would like to assist change.

  o Do not make your personal agenda all about you, because the world is not revolving around you. You need to be the agent of change somewhere in the world.

- ○ Make sure that if you died today, somebody would miss you because of your generous heart. Don't die without knowing your legacy. Where did you make a difference in the world?

Step 2: Become the Insider

Tony Robbins suggests that each of us take up control of our budgetary future and plot a goal to success, by being proactive in our money management. He emphasizes we need to learn the rules of the game. He suggests that we don't make investment decisions until we have studied where the money goes.

When Tony asks where the money goes, this is a twofold question. He wants to know where in your personal finances the money goes out of your household accounts, and he wants to know where the money flows from your investment accounts to your account managers.

There are two periods of money management, accumulation and decumulation. In the accumulation period you gather wealth, in the decumulation period you live off the interest and returns. This book addresses both periods of money management, but emphasizes the former most. By closely examining all of our spending patterns, we can determine where we are wasteful and where we can improve our investment performance.

Myths of Financial Money Management that rob us of the savings we have invested.

- *Invest with us and we'll beat the market.* Most of these firms have high load front end fees that eat up your capital and increase their gains. Every firm will pick a winner once in a while, but the ones that are self-promoting are usually promoting their own pockets. Avoid allowing a financial planner to determine your investment decisions. Inform yourself daily about the market and base your decisions on your store of information.

- *The mutual fund industry is the world's largest skimming operating, taking money from every investor at an alarming rate because of their high fees to the clients.* To know the true amount that your portfolio is costing, search your investments on the website *Personal Fund* (https://www.personalcapital. com/financial-software/fee-analyzer). Seek a mutual fund, if you still choose to use this type of investment that has the lowest fees and the highest rate of return on investment.

- *Investment firms rearrange the numbers to use statistics to put spin on the results.* What they say isn't necessarily what is the actual bottom line of return. Thoroughly research each investment in your portfolio, asking for the complete series of ROI reports, not just the blurb that is sent at the end of the company newsletter.

- *I'm your broker and I'm here to help [you pay for my daughter's new car with your investment fees].* To receive financial advice free of conflicts of interest, sign with a fiduciary. They are required by law to disclose all their financial associations. *Stronghold Financial* (https://www.strongholdfinancial.com) will assess all your investments and give 5 free tips to making more returns for free on their website. Most firms charge $1,000 or more for this task. Take advantage of this offer to see where you can make more money with less loaded fees.

- *Your retirement [needs will be met if you buy into our 401(k)] is just a 401(k) away.* This is misleading information as it does not take into account the fees that that are lost in your 401(k) every year. Checking with the *Fee Checker* (http://americas-best401k.com/fee-checker) will unveil the true cost of your 401(k) fees. After you have entered your 401(k) and received the information, consider transferring your 401(k), at no cost to you, to a lower fee and higher return fund manager.

- *Target date funds tout "just set it and forget it," hoping you will forget their high cost of management.* A target date fund is one in which you list the target date of your retirement and they invest the funds accordingly as to risk and exposure investing. The target date firm will promote high risk investments for young people, mid risk for middle aged persons, and low risk or bonds for the elderly about to retire.

- *I hate annuities and you should, too.* This is misleading advice because the risk-taking annuities are the variable annuities, fixed indexed annuities can give you a high income with a guarantee of no-risk. Fixed indexed annuities earn a specific fixed rate of interest that is a guarantee by the insurance company managing the fund, or the interest rate is based on the growth rate of an external index and will still be guaranteed by the insurance company.

- *You have to take huge risks to gain big rewards, [an excuse for spending down your capital].* There are investments like structured notes that will pay great returns, but they must be searched for diligently. Market-Linked CD's include FDIC insurance for your investment. Fixed Indexed Annuities are another safe, high return investment. Due diligence is required in researching these funds also, as other annuities appear to give a better rate, then eat up your capital by charging high transfer fees.

- *The lies we tell ourselves.* We base more of our decisions on our internal dialogue that from external advice. Our fear of failure keeps us from moving forward in our financial path to success. We erroneously buy into the idea that small investing is worse than no investing, as it gives small balances and small returns. We have bought the idea of "go big or not at all." Even saving just $2,000 annually, which is only $38.50 weekly (pizza for a family of 4), will yield $102,320.00 at 8%, compounding daily for 20 years. How many weeks have you blown off $40 for dinner and didn't think twice? If you had saved only that much for the week, in twenty years of compound interest at 8% you would have over $100,000. You probably told yourself this was not worth saving because it wasn't very much money. Skip the pizza or the dinner out and go for the savings immediately.

STEP 3: MAKE THE GAME WINNABLE

These three cognitive breakthroughs are necessary to make the most out of your investments and financial goals. Changes in our attitudes are important. These changes are the kick start to fulfilling our financial dreams and goals.

If you want to change your life you have to change your

- **strategy** by valuing yourself and your commitment to savings and investing,

- **your story** to no longer think of yourself as a victim in a hand to mouth existence,

- **and your state of being** by taking control of your body and your health.

You have to leap and move into the investing mode instead of the "getting by" mode. You have to change the way you think of your success, no longer in the conspicuous consumer "success shows: mode and instead in the "I am powerful and in control" mode. You also have to change the way you view yourself. This includes looking at your physical health and lifestyle because it doesn't help to accumulate wealth and then immediately die. Change all your immediate patterns into long-term growth and sustenance mode that focuses on long-term objectives and goals.

Robbins identified **Five Basic Financial Dreams**, which one is yours?

1. **Financial Security**, means that without having to work another day, you still have enough income to pay for your home, food, utilities, transportation and insurance.

2. **Financial Vitality**, having enough for extras and half your expenses covered without working.

3. **Financial Independence**, maintaining the standard of living you desire without additional work.

4. **Financial Freedom**, living the lifestyle, having extras, and still not having to work.

5. **Absolute Financial Freedom**, the ability to have whatever you want and still not having to work.

To achieve your financial dream you need:

- to **focus** on the goal, with a dedicated plan of intent

- to initiate **massive action**, utilizing your saving strategies now instead of putting them off until the right time or enough money

- **Grace**, knowing that you have been blessed, which instills an attitude of gratitude, and eliminates the victim mentality that can pull you down.

Recap:

1. Save more and invest, live on less and simplify, pare your budget and make saving the number one priority in all financial spending. No longer accept self-talk and excuses that sabotage your financial goals.

2. Save 50% of income so that you become in control of future, reduce debt and other financial obligations so you can save 50%, live on less and like it more with gratitude. Money is the tool to your financial freedom but will not give you freedom if you continue to spend rather than save industriously.

3. Reduce taxes and fees legally by hiring a CPA well versed in tax cut savings, Roth and 401k savings plans work to build savings as long as you regularly invest in them, examine each progress report in your 401(k) and look at how much you are

paying in financial transaction and management fees. Move these monies to a broker that has lower fees and a higher return. Make this money work for you.

4. Diversify investments, don't put everything in one type of investment, use bonds for down financial markets, purchase stocks on up markets, buy property for leverage and collateral. Look at your entire portfolio and apportion the investments to survive economic changes.

5. If you can't save at least 50% of your income, take a second job just to invest. Whether it is a paper route or a freelance consulting position, put all of this income into your investments as if you never earned this money.

Step 4: Focus on the Most Important Decision

There are three tools for reducing your risks and creating financial success:

1. Stock Selection

2. Market Timing and,

3. Asset Allocation.

Of these, the paramount decision is where to place your asset allocation, or where to place your money for the best returns on investment. Asset allocation does not just mean to diversify your portfolio; it means to invest your assets on the right investment opportunities, at the correct time. Doing this will assure you meet your financials goals with assurance within the timeframe that you have allotted. This requires that you work to obtain the crucial knowledge needed to wisely handle your investments. Do your homework, don't allow an investment advisor to make your financial decisions for you.

Study the financial pages every day. Follow the stock market, the bond market, the local real estate market, the commodities market, the price of gold, stock indexing and anything else that is in your portfolio. Devote at least 2 hours a day in analyzing the current financial markets. If you want your money to perform to your goal standards, you need to perform the due diligence required. Your new job is financial advisor for yourself and your investment portfolio. Don't give your money and your power to a broker or financial manager. You are the best decision maker for your funds, so must educate yourself and stay informed on the financial markets. Learn to get the best returns and reduced fees.

Your securities bucket should include, but not be limited to:

Cash - you need an emergency fund that is liquid and equal to six months' living expenses, plus the cash to purchase what you need for impulse buys or your hobbies.

Bonds - these are for the down market, a percentage of your portfolio should be utilized in bonds for those recession and depression market times.

CDs - place these with your local bank to invest in your home-town and build local goodwill.

Your home - with a good interest rate, your home payment could be less than rent and give you a nicer place to live, while also increasing your asset portfolio.

Your pension - paid by your employer when you take full advantage of your 401(k).

Your annuities - you have chosen the fixed rate annuities that provide a specific payout.

Your life insurance - you have paid a life insurance policy that is whole life and at a fixed rate. You need to provide cash for your family at your burial because the immediate expenses can be over $10,000, and most of them are due at your death.

Your structured notes - they can pay returns annually that you can reinvest, giving you a double-win situation.

STEP 5: CREATE A LIFELONG PLAN

Robbins suggests utilizing the All Seasons approach when creating your lifelong plan for investment strategies. The All Seasons, sometimes called All Weather approach is defined below:

Ray Dalio's All Seasons Approach

1. Inflation - Inflation is defined as a general increase in prices while at the same time decreasing the value of the dollar. Suggested purchases during inflationary times are: TIPS, (treasury inflation protected securities), gold and commodities.

2. Deflation - Deflation is a sign that economic growth is deteriorating. In a deflationary period, prices will fall, unemployment goes up and production decreases unemployment will rise, and production goes down. As deflation continues the stock market will drop, credit will be tightened, and cash will be hoarded by businesses concerned with their negative sales and decreasing market share. Good purchases during deflationary times are: stocks and treasury bonds.

3. Rising Economic Growth - Rising economic growth is what everybody wants. Rising economic growth means the increase in production and the standard of living for the majority of the population. Economic growth is based on the country's Gross Domestic Product per capita or GNP, usually increased by an advance in technology. Suggested purchases in times of rising economic growth: stocks, corporate bonds, gold, and commodities.

4. Decreasing Economic Growth - Decreasing economic growth means that production goes down. Good invest-

ments in a period of decreasing economic growth are: Treasury bonds and TIPS.

The story of the All Weather portfolio by Ray Dalio is this: Ray incorrectly gauged the public's reaction to President Nixon's announcement that he was increasing the currency supply in the United States' economy. The result of Nixon's announcement was an increase in the value of gold. Ray was only 20 and called this market fluctuation incorrectly, causing a decrease in his portfolio value. Ray realized that a lifetime of knowledge wasn't enough to anticipate market fluctuations, so he developed his All-Weather investment principle. The primary focus of the All Weather, also called the All Seasons approach to investing, is:

An investment portfolio that performs well given any economic environment or fluctuations in existence. The brainstormers at Bridgewater, Associates developed the following plan to assure quality performance in all investment, even when the economy and financial markets are fluctuating. Even the savviest investor cannot predict all of the market changes due to the global economy. It would take hundreds of hours to personally watch each country and each war zone and the weather and production of commodities, diamond brokers, gold bouillon, etc. The best way to ensure that your money is both safe and working hard is to allocate your investments into separate seasons, each with a specific purpose.

The first strategy is to **divide your investment portfolio into 4ths.** Take a closer look at immediate annuities and deferred annuities to pad your portfolio for long term dividends. Examine the bond market and bond indexes. Pick some stocks that pay dividend checks and pick some stocks that double and triple and then split, giving you double or triple value and redemption. Bonds have the same types of income. Some pay annual dividends and others retain their value but pay out at double what you paid in when the redemption day comes. Pick the ones that coincide with your personal investment goals and increase their presence in your portfolio over time.

The All Seasons portfolio will ideally be constructed of the following investments.

30% in **stocks** that have proven growth, also known as blue-chip stocks,

15% in **intermediate bonds** such as this list on *Morningstar.com* (http://news.morningstar.com/fund-category-returns/intermediate-term-bond/$FOCA$CI.aspx) and

40% in **long term bonds**, top returns are found on this list at Morningstar.com (http://news.morningstar.com/fund-category-returns/long-term-bond/$FOCA$CL.aspx)

7.5% in **gold**, current gold prices can be located here at kitco.com (http://www.kitco.com/market)

7.5% in **commodities**, current commodities performance can be found here at nasdaq.com (http://www.nasdaq.com/markets/commodities.aspx)

Stocks are better purchased in transactions of 100, known as blocks, or in a mutual fund. Search your stocks so that you are aware of the market price, and set your purchase with a limit. You will have a choice of purchasing through a full-service broker or a discount broker. Most full-service brokers require a $50,000 deposit, and charge a much higher service fee. However, for these fees they will hold your hand and walk you through your investment transactions. A discount broker may accept $1,000 as a minimum balance. They give no hand holding whatsoever, but they also charge minimal fees to handle your transactions. Be very aware that when you place your order the money is gone from your hands to his, there is no turning back. Stock trades usually cost a minimum of 5% to buy or sell, so if your total transaction has a yield of less than 10% profit, you have lost money before even checking the stock value.

Bonds can be purchased online in minimal amounts from Treasury

Direct (http://www.treasurydirect.gov). Here you can buy your TIPS (Treasury Inflation-Protected Securities), savings bonds, etc. TIPS are offered in 5, 10, and 30-year maturities and sold in increments of $100. The price and maturity rate of the TIPS is a price set on the day of the auction.

When you purchase a TIPS, the treasury charges you accrued interest for the time that you own the security. The Treasury Direct pays you back that interest later semiannually.

The interest accrued on TIPS start on the 15th of the month. However, they are not issued until the end of the month on the last business day. If you have an original issue of TIPS, the interest is accrued and payable from the 15th until the end of the month when it was issued. For TIPS that are reopened, the interest is paid from the date of the announcement right up to the date the reopening date of the issued TIPS.

Treasury Direct will deduct the price of the TIPS and any interest accrued from your primary bank account. To determine how much each TIPS will cost do the following:

1. On the day of the auction, after 5 PM eastern time, search for your Pending Transaction Details, under Current Holdings.

2. Check the price per $100.

3. Add the accrued interest amount.

4. Make sure the amount is available from your account before the issue date.

Gold is purchased from precious metals dealers and exchanges. Gold bullion can be bought in coins, gold bars, and jewelry. Gold is a low risk investment and a hedge against inflation.

Gold coins are more valuable if they were minted before 1933, as they can be sold in two arenas, coin collectors and the commodities markets. The British Sovereign and the American Eagle are 22 karat gold. Other gold coins like the Canadian Maple Leaf have at least 91% gold content. In the same 91% realm you'll find the Krugerrand from South Africa, and the Kangaroo from Australia. The Austrian Philharmonic coin is 24 karat gold.

Gold bars are 99.5 to 99.9% pure gold. The manufacturer is stamped on the bars. Known quality manufacturers are PAMP, Credit Suisse, Johnson Mathey, and Metalor.

Gold jewelry is an iffy proposition for collectors. Jewelry that is made of 14 karat or less is not worth purchasing for the gold content. Jewelry that is intricately designed is usually collected for its beauty as well, and may be priced accordingly by the seller. The best place to purchase gold jewelry for the content is estate sales and estate auctions. These places may have vintage pieces that may not hold interest for the common bidder.

Commodities investing is a highly volatile market that can make big gains or big losses in a microsecond. The advantage of commodities investing in a well-balanced portfolio is the commodities gains can offset the stock market losses, as long as funds are not heavily invested and risked by the savvy consumer. Purchasing commodities can be achieved through mutual funds and commodities funds, or they can be purchased individually by the investor. Be sure to place stops and define exactly what you are willing to risk or pay for commodities shares. Don't remove the stops in hopes the commodity will rebound. Stops are placed there for a reason. Remember Warren Buffet's number 1 and number 2 rules of investing, Don't lose money.

Wise advice from a commodities broker: the only person who always wins on commodities trading is the broker. The broker gets fees from both the buyer and the seller. Get used to losing in commodities trades, it is very easy to lose money in a single trade.

STEP 6: INVEST LIKE THE .001%

As Warren Buffet says of investing, "Rule number 1 is: Don't lose money, Rule number 2 is, Don't forget rule number 1." If you have an investment with a poor performance return, yank that investment immediately and substitute a better investment. Don't throw good money after bad and don't hang on to your bad investment out of pride or hope things will turn around. Waiting on an investment to mature is like waiting for an apple to ripen, it might mature into a sweet product, or it just might rot instead.

Only choose the risk level in which you are comfortable. No matter how tempting the high return stocks are to your asset collection, don't invest your money in high risk investments if you are not comfortable losing that money overnight. High return investments are by nature high risk. Building your portfolio should be about accumulation of assets at this point, not taking high risks in the hopes of increasing wealth on the fast track. This is your long-term investment plan. Don't throw off your plan by using greedy tactics for investing.

Keep studying and learning every day about your portfolio and money management. Invest in your knowledge about financial markets. Dedicate daily study sessions of the market and returns. Look up all your funds and reassess their performance and value. Don't be lazy and allow funds managers to do the hard work of tracking the funds, engage the markets on a regular basis. Read the financial news in the Wall Street Journal and online publications. Investigate various markets to see the trends. Speculate on a particular stock by watching it daily to track the performance. Consider buying index funds or mutual funds that include this particular stock to reap the upwards trend.

Recap:

- Buy mutual and index funds, not small amounts of individual stocks. When you buy stocks, buy a minimum of 100 shares at a time. Invest in a CPA so that you can reap the tax advantages. See if these stock purchases qualify for exemption 338 of the tax code, *Treating a Stock Purchase as an Asset Acquisition* (https://www.law.cornell.edu/uscode/text/26/338).

- Only poor people invest in gold as a primary asset. These people are purchasing gold as protection against a total economic collapse. This is the "prepper" mentality, a type of victim mentality and survival strategy. Keep your portfolio to 7.5% gold investments and invest in America's growth, not its demise.

- Look at high return closed ended funds, they may yield as much as 9%. Examine your information closely to assure there are no front-end fee loads or high participant fees. Look at how they use market leverage, it affects the performance of the fund but also may have a high-risk ratio.

- Don't look for the next big thing, you won't find it. Stay in your field of expertise when investing. Don't search for the newest, hottest, super flashy investment funds that promise high yields. Instead, research the steady performers which you can feel confident with their products and services, and stick with them. Investing in the hottest thing will burn your fingers if they crash and burn, dropping fast and leaving unsuspecting investors with a worthless stock.

- Look at equities of all kinds, a type of stock that represents ownership investment. These equities can be public or private stocks, and will give a return on investment based on the corporate earnings. Research particularly financial, technology, exchange traded, and consumer equities to determine where they fit in your portfolio.

STEP 7: JUST DO IT, ENJOY IT, AND SHARE IT

Even though this entire book is about money, Anthony Robbins is emphatic in his conclusion that dwelling on money will only bring you temporary happiness, not financial security, and certainly not a joyful life. Tony says that a life focused on money and wealth is an unhappy person that will not achieve financial success. This person's emotional neediness will undermine his desire for financial security.

Robbins ultimate focus is about being real, enjoying the life you have, and losing the worry and concern that surrounds money. His primary points are:

- Life is not all about money- if you get mesmerized by accumulating wealth for the sake of having the biggest bank account, you've missed the whole point of this book. Robbins relates many examples of how money by itself is just an instrument to give you stability and alleviate your worries and anxieties.

- Life is about love, caring, and relationships - Robbins comments that the bottom line is who you love, how you show you care, and taking time away from earning money to have satisfying and nurturing relationships. If making money and building your portfolio is the only way you receive joy and satisfaction, you have your priorities mixed up. The portfolio is the passport to freedom from financial worries. The portfolio is not the purveyor of joy or happiness; it is a means to an end.

- Money is only a tool to help you get satisfaction in life - it is not the destination. Life is a journey of ups and downs, trials and tribulations. Money is a means to make the journey easier, but it is not the point of life. The point of life is to love and be loved. Money in the bank can give you the freedom to love, but it won't buy you love, unless you buy a dog.

- We can't take our money with us when we die - many people have tried and there just isn't a way to take the money with us. This means we need to enjoy each day for the grace that we have been given, the gifts we are allowed to steward, and the friendships and connections we have made in love and relationship. Every day is a gift from the Creator, no matter what you call the Creator. We didn't make this day ourselves and we have no guarantees for tomorrow. Wake up each morning joyful that you are alive and breathing. Find a way to give happiness every day to someone else. Nurture someone, love someone, and bring a positive attitude to the day. Death is the great equalizer. Everyone fits in the same sized coffin and the same burial plot.

  - Make sure your family and those you care for are well provided for when you are gone. Make out a will today, naming gifts and funds, where they are to be disbursed and how you want them allocated. Don't assume you will live forever because you will not. If you don't have life insurance, buy a policy now. Make it a whole life policy if you can so that it will accrue interest when you have paid it in full. Don't fall for the trap of term life insurance, those rates can double overnight.

- What matters is the time we've had with the people we love, the things we've done that made us feel alive, and the impact we've had on the world.

  - Take the time to spend time with your loved ones. Designate a time and place to weekly share a meal and your thoughts. Turn off the phones and electronics, even if it means you have to go to the country every week and picnic at the lake. When you're gone, those will be the memorable times, not the times you're watching TV.

  - What are the things that make you feel alive? It is traveling? Set aside part of your savings to enjoy the beauty of nature, or the theatre, or the orchestral performances. Do what matters to you and what thrills your soul. We only have one journey, so make it count. Determine the most important things that nurture your spirit and spirituality, and invest your time, energy and money on these items. Don't waste precious minutes doing what is boring, dull, and mundane. Don't spend time with negative people that pull you down, instead surround yourself with positive, like-minded people that will nurture you.

○ What impact have you had on the world? If you can't identify it immediately, it is time for self-examination. What is the mark you want to leave for humanity? How do you want to create your immortality? Do you want to protect the whales? Create a legacy with a fund for whale protection or whale studies. Do you want to impact education? Create a fund that provides computers to third word citizens or the working poor in the United States. Pick an elementary school and provide the funding for an entire class to have an iPad for schoolwork. Invest in technology and people at the same time.

○ What will your personal contribution to the betterment of mankind be? Will you help underwrite undersea exploration? Does space exploration excite you? What about the tropical rain forests? Do you want to help eliminate cancer? Maybe you will choose something even closer to home, like decorate a wing at your local hospital or pay for one person's cancer treatments? It may be only affordable for you to help one person, but to that one person you are the face of God that has given them a miracle. Be a miracle worker for your legacy.

CONCLUSION

Thank you again for downloading this book! I hope this book was able to help you to create a successful plan for Financial Freedom.

The next step is to stop planning and start saving and investing.

Thank you for reading!

Dear Reader,

I hope you enjoyed **Summary: Money Master the Game**. I have to tell you I really love Tony Robbins' books and programs.

When I wrote the **Summary: Money Master the Game**, I got so many letters thanking me for the book. Some love the step by step action guide, and others just love the easy read and quick reminder of the key points to be able to take action. As an author, I love feedback.

Candidly, you are the reason that I will explore future books and turn them into actionable and time limited challenges for your personal use. So, tell me what you liked, what you loved, even what you hated. I'd love to hear from you.

Finally, I need to ask a favor. If you're so inclined, I'd love a review of this book. Loved it, hated it--I'd just enjoy your feedback.

As you me have gleaned from my book, reviews can be tough to come by these days. You, the reader, have the power now to make or break a book. If you have the time, please leave a review on Amazon.

Thank you so much for reading and for spending time with me.

In gratitude,

Mike Faiola

REFERENCES

Anand Chokkavelu, C. (2015). *How to Never Lose Money.* [online]
Fool.com. Available at: http://www.fool.com/investing/
value/2010/03/30/how-to-never-lose-money.aspx [Accessed 8
Oct. 2015].

Dalio, R. (2015). *The All Weather Story: How Bridgewater
Associates Created the All Weather Investment Strategy, the
Foundation of the 'Risk Parity' Movement..* 1st ed. [ebook]
Westport, CT: Bridgewater Associates, pp.1-6. Available at:
http://www.bwater.com/Uploads/FileManager/research/All-
Weather/All-Weather-Story.pdf [Accessed 8 Oct. 2015].

Investmentnews.com, (2015). *The path to financial freedom -Tony
Robbins' 7 steps to financial freedom.* [online] Available
at: http://www.investmentnews.com/gallery/20141116/
FREE/111409999/PH/tony-robbins-7-steps-to-financial-freedom
[Accessed 4 Oct. 2015].

Robbins, A. (n.d.). *Money.*

Made in United States
North Haven, CT
16 May 2025